EMBROIDERY

EMBROIDERY

Jennifer Rollins

CRESCENT BOOKS

NEW YORK • AVENEL, NEW JERSEY

Special thanks to Anne Docker, Jenny Johnson and Monika Kaatzke

This 1994 edition published by Crescent Books,
distributed by Random House Value Publishing, Inc.,
40 Engelhard Avenue, Avenel, New Jersey 07001.

Random House
New York • Toronto • London • Sydney • Auckland

First published in 1992
Reprinted in 1993
Reprinted in 1994

Publishing Manager: Robin Burgess
Project Coordinator: Mary Moody
Editor: Dulcie Andrews
Illustrator: Kathie Baxter Smith
Designed & produced for the publisher by Phillip Mathews Publishers
Typeset in the U.K. by Seller's
Produced in Singapore by Imago

Title: Country Crafts Series: Embroidery
ISBN: 0 517 10252 8

CONTENTS

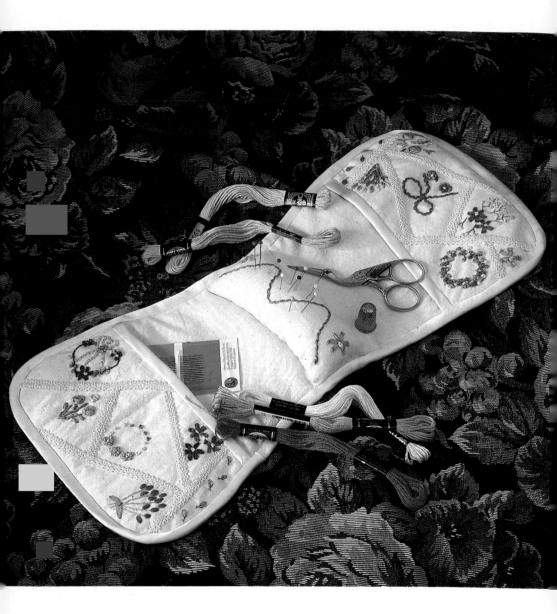

An embroidered sewing purse holds threads, needles, scissors and thimbles.

INTRODUCTION

Through this Country Craft series, it is our hope that you will find satisfaction and enjoyment in learning a new skill. In this case, that of embroidery.

The creative pleasures of needlecraft, and embroidery in particular, have been known for centuries and the embellishment of such items as clothing, furniture, curtains and tablecloths has always been a favorite domestic activity.

As with many other traditional crafts, embroidery has undergone something of a revival in the last few decades, with an ever increasing number of kit projects, design transfers and new thread styles and colors. Many of the ready-to-embroider projects, however, concentrate on one particular stitch, such as cross stitch or long stitch, to create the design. While this is fine for the beginner, the serious embroiderer may soon lose interest.

This book provides you with advice on how to design, make and finish off your own freestyle embroidery projects and includes a stitch guide which takes you step-by-step through a wide range of useful and attractive embroidery stitches. There is also a simple beginner's project to start you off and give you confidence in your newly acquired embroidery skills.

A beautifully designed and embroidered cushion.

THE HISTORY OF EMBROIDERY

EMBROIDERY has a long and complex history that in many ways mirrors the history of the societies from which it developed. Evidence that stitching with needle and thread in some form or other was employed as early as 3000BC comes from the discovery of bone and bronze needles.

The earliest examples of true embroidery come from fabrics found in Coptic graves dating from around the 1st century AD and represent embroidery in its simplest forms, running stitch, cross stitch and back stitch in simple patterns used to decorate the rough linen used for burial wear.

Knot, satin and chain stitches, found on fabric from countries as diverse as Russia and Greece, testify to the complex trade connections that existed in the ancient world. China, too, has a long history of embroidery, with a number of examples of intricately worked flowers, fruit and landscape scenes in a great variety of stitches, in a good state of preservation a thousand years after their creation.

The oldest surviving English embroidery comes from the 10th century AD, a cloak executed in silver gilt thread and colored silks and designed for use as a church vestment. While poorly preserved, it nonetheless demonstrates the high degree of skill already practiced by embroidery artisans of this period.

Secular embroidery, often commissioned by knights or noblemen to depict particular events in which they were involved, used less expensive threads and simpler stitches but was full of life and vigor. The most famous of these embroideries is the Bayeux Tapestry, executed in laid and couched work with running stitches used as outlines. It was made by a group of English artisans in the 11th century and depicts, in a 230 feet long sequence, the Norman conquest of England.

Opus anglicanum (English work) refers to a particular style of embroidery, practiced by English craftsmen from the 13th century onwards. It was famous for its originality of design, variety and fineness of its stitches, and the costliness of its materials, which included pearls, jewels, silks and gold and silver threads. Many examples remain of this work, which was highly prized by both the churches and monarchs of Europe.

From the 14th to the 16th century, the quality of ecclesiastical embroidery declined. A reliance on brocades and appliqué took the place of intricate embroidery, less time-consuming stitches were used and the overall effect was coarser.

The 16th century saw a revival of interest in domestic embroidery. Fine running stitch was used to embroider linen shirts and, because

this stitch is often seen on the clothing in Holbein portraits, it has become known as Holbein stitch.

Embroidery pattern books also became immensely popular during this period so that many designs were available for different types of embroidery, particularly for counted thread embroidery which could be printed in chart form.

At the same time, a general domestic interest in flower gardens, as opposed to the purely utilitarian herb or vegetable garden, led to an upsurge in embroidery patterns based on flowers and leaves. A design of scrolling stems encircling flower heads was especially popular. Roses, cornflowers, honeysuckle, leaves, pea pods, caterpillars and butterflies were all used as design elements on shirt sleeves, coifs, purses and pincushions, to name just a few of the items covered with embroidery of this type.

Trade links with India and China also influenced embroidery patterns and the artisans and domestic embroiderers of France and Germany in particular used pagodas, crane-like birds and exotic fruits, flowers and animals in their work. The Baroque and Rococo periods also embraced these particular design features and pomegranates, passion flowers and chinoiserie abounded.

Making an embroidery sampler was part of a young girl's education and many exist from the 16th century onwards. Either worked in bands or randomly over the fabric, the sampler contained a great variety of stitches, many of which are found only on samplers, having fallen out of favor as decoration for clothing or furnishings.

Embroidery as a primarily leisure activity was not really practiced until the 19th century. Whitework (white stitching on a white background), smocking and Berlin woolwork (a charted, counted thread embroidery style in bright colors) all became very popular as crafts for well-to-do women, although banal designs and a limited variety of stitches often resulted in work of inferior quality.

This century has seen a revival of interest in traditional embroidery styles. Northern European folk embroidery, with its emphasis on geometric, cross-stitched designs in one or two colors has become very popular, no doubt in part because it is easy to replicate and chart the designs. The establishment of embroidery guilds has served to inform and educate embroiderers about traditional techniques and as a result, styles such as blackwork and cutwork have been revived and revitalized.

Parallel with this revival, however, has been an interest in entirely contemporary embroidery techniques where, for example, embroidery has been combined with other techniques such as appliqué, beading and collage work to create very modern works of art. Machine embroidery has also become popular, with many machines offering a wide range of complicated stitches.

Opposite: A charming pin cushion using bullion stitch, French knots and satin stitch variations.

Tools and equipment.

TOOLS AND MATERIALS

AS WITH MANY of the traditional needlecrafts, embroidery is a craft that requires only a few items; needle, thread and fabric being the most important. Nevertheless, there is a wide choice of materials available to modern embroiderers and it is necessary to understand the differences between them before you can decide which materials are suited to the particular project you have in mind. Some threads for example, are designed to be used with certain types of fabrics. Some fabrics should only be used when doing particular kinds of embroidery and so on.

The intended function of a piece of embroidery will also dictate which materials you choose. Embroidery used to decorate an item of clothing should be executed in threads which will wash in the same way as the background fabric, otherwise you will have to dry clean the item each time it gets dirty. On the other hand, if you are making a decorative sampler designed for use as a wall hanging, you will be much less restricted in your thread and fabric choices.

THREADS

There is a huge range of threads on the market, from ultra fine silks to sturdy cottons and wools. The color possibilities are also almost unlimited, from delicate pastels to bright, vibrant colors with every hue in between. Also available are metallic threads in gold and silver as well as other shades such as red, blue and green.

Embroidery threads can also be further categorized by whether they are divisible or not. Divisible threads are made up of two or more finer strands that may be pulled apart and used separately, which gives you the choice of using a thicker or thinner version of the same thread, depending on the weight of the fabric you are using and the effect you want to create.

Stranded cotton or Embroidery thread
This is the most widely used of the embroidery threads and comes in a large range of colors and is also divisible for fine work. It is suitable for most kinds of embroidery.

Pearlized cotton
Available in different weights, Nos. 5 and 8 being the most popular. No. 5 is used for counted thread embroidery, while No. 8 is widely used for cutwork, although it is suitable for most medium to fine embroidery stitches. It is non-divisible.

"Soft" or matt embroidery cotton
This thread has a matte finish, is non-divisible and is used for bold stitches on heavier fabric.

Broder cotton (*coton à broder*)
A thread with a lustrous finish. It is used as a single thread for cutwork, drawn thread and drawn fabric work.

Crewel wool
A fine woollen thread suited to both free-

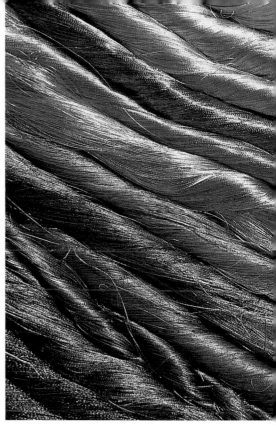

There are hundreds of thread colors and texture combinations from which to choose.

15

style and counted thread embroidery. It can be used as a single strand, or between two to four strands may be combined for heavier weight fabrics.

Persian wool

A divisible woollen thread which comes in a large range of bright colors.

Tapestry (*tapisserie* or gobelin) wool

This is the thickest of all the threads and is used for working on canvas tapestries.

Do not use knitting wool for embroidery as it may fray or pull apart as it is drawn through the fabric.

Specialty needlework stores also carry a range of other yarns, such as silks, synthetic threads, metallic threads and other textured threads for creating special effects. It is possible to create interesting effects of your own by combining two or more different strands of thread. This is especially useful in creating a particular shade of color that is not catered for in the standard range.

NEEDLES

Crewel and chenille needles are used for free-style embroidery.

Crewel needles

These needles are long and sharp and are used with plain weave fabrics and fine to medium weight threads.

Chenille needles

Also pointed, but these needles have a larger eye to accommodate thicker threads.

Tapestry needles

Needles which have a blunt end instead of a point. They are used with even weave and canvas fabrics in counted thread embroidery where the needle must pass through the holes between the fabric strands, rather than splitting the strands.

FABRICS

There are three categories of fabrics when considering embroidery, plain (or common) weave, even weave and canvas. Canvas work is considered to be a craft all on its own and therefore will not be discussed here.

Plain weave

This is the name given to most tightly woven fabrics with a smooth surface. Examples include linen, cotton, hessian and silk, as well as some of the synthetic fabrics. Very loosely woven, knitted or stretch fabrics are not suitable for embroidery because of their tendency to pucker and pull out of shape as the embroidery progresses.

Some plain weaves have a pattern either woven into or printed onto the fabric. If the pattern is spaced evenly, such as with gingham or polka dots, it may be used as a stitching guide for such embroidery stitches as cross stitch or smocking.

Even weave

Even weave fabrics are those which have the same number of threads running horizontally and vertically. The number of threads per 1 inch, or thread count, indicates the tightness or fineness of the weave. A thread count of eighteen therefore indicates a fabric of finer weave than one with a thread count of nine. There are many even weave materials especially designed for embroidery, including fabrics which have pairs of threads and fabrics, which have blocks of four tightly woven threads running horizontally and vertically in a basketweave pattern. Also available is single weave fabric in both coarse and fine weaves.

SCISSORS

A pair of good quality embroidery scissors is

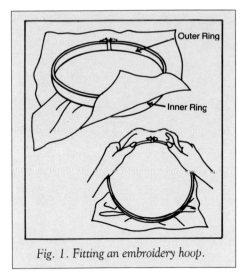

Fig. 1. Fitting an embroidery hoop.

to remove the work when you have finished sewing for the day. For added protection, bind the inner circle with cotton tape before inserting the fabric. To prevent squashing of stitches already worked, place a layer of acid-free tissue paper over the top of the fabric before positioning the outer ring of the hoop. After the screw of the hoop has been tightened, expose the work by tearing away the tissue paper in the middle of the hoop (see Fig. 2).

Embroidery frames are designed to hold the entire work all at once. There are some very sophisticated frames on the market, but you can make a perfectly adequate frame from four pieces of timber, mitered at the corners, which are joined together to make a square or rectangular shape. The embroidery is then stapled to the timber frame with an even, firm tension and is kept on this frame until the work is complete (see Fig. 3).

essential. Make sure that the blades are sharp and that they have pointed ends for snipping and trimming.

EMBROIDERY HOOPS and FRAMES

Even if you are able to keep your sewing tension very even, fabric has a tendency to pucker and distort when covered with areas of closely worked stitching. The best way to prevent this is to use an embroidery hoop, which will keep the fabric taut and the warp and weft at right angles to each other. A hoop is constructed of two circles of wood or metal or plastic, one fitting snugly inside the other. The fabric is laid over the inner circle, while the outer circle, which is fitted with a screw that allows it to be tightened or loosened, is placed over the top. By tightening the screw the fabric is gradually pulled taut and held in shape while you work. (see Fig. 1).

The embroidery should not be left in the hoop for long periods and it is a good policy

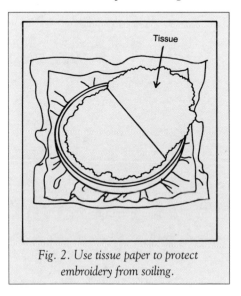

Fig. 2. Use tissue paper to protect embroidery from soiling.

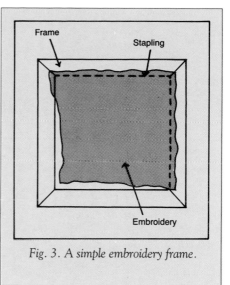

Fig. 3. A simple embroidery frame.

OTHER TOOLS and MATERIALS

There are a number of other items that you may find useful. If you are comfortable using one, a thimble can be helpful in guiding the needle through the fabric. Some embroiderers find needle threaders a boon, others would be lost without a magnifying glass that hangs around the neck, leaving both hands free to embroider. At the design and transfer stage of the embroidery, pencils, tracing paper, colored pens or paints, graph paper, a ruler and transfer pencils are all useful tools.

A precise satin stitch has been used to create the main part of the design on this embroidered tablecloth.

A delicate white-on-white embroidered cushion.

STARTING WORK

PREPARING THE FABRIC

The fabric should be washed in warm, soapy water to eliminate the possibility of shrinkage later on, and well ironed, since creasing could interfere with stitch tension.

Cut the fabric as least 3 inches larger than the size of the finished design, although if you intend to frame the work you will need to add 5 inches all around to allow for the framing process. Machine or hand-hem around the edges of the fabric to prevent fraying.

Finally, locate the center point of the fabric by folding it in half horizontally and then vertically, pressing in the folds with a finger.

The point at which the two folds intersect is the center. Mark this with a pencil or fabric marker. This will help you later on when you are transferring the design to the fabric.

TRANSFERRING DESIGNS

While there are many attractive embroidery projects available in kit form, it can also be very satisfying to create your own design.

If you have a particular design that you want to use, there are a number of ways of transferring designs to your background fabric.

Carbon paper   The first method uses dressmaker's carbon paper. Place the carbon paper, inked side down, onto the fabric. Place the design over the top of the carbon paper, making sure that it is centered over the fabric, and then pin all three layers together to prevent shifting. With a tracing wheel, trace firmly over the design.

If the design is very complicated, a knitting pin used as a pencil will give you more control when tracing.

Light box   A light box is another way of transferring the design and is best suited to fine fabrics. A light box simply consists of a light source behind a piece of glass.

The design is taped onto the glass, the fabric is taped over the top and when the light is turned on, the design becomes visible through the fabric. The design is then traced onto the fabric with pencil or fabric marker.

A window, a glass-topped table or even the television with the channel selector off a station, can be used as a light box.

Tissue paper   For fabrics with a pile or uneven surface, drawing the design can be difficult. In this case, trace the design onto tissue paper and pin the paper to the fabric.

In a contrasting thread and with small stitches, tack around the design, taking care to include all angles and small details. Pull away the tissue paper, leaving the design tacked on the fabric.

Transfer pencil   This transfer technique uses a transfer pencil. Trace your design onto tracing paper with a transfer pencil, available from craft stores. Place the design face down onto the fabric and cover with a hot iron for a few seconds. The design will transfer from the tracing paper to the fabric.

This method is only suited to those fabrics that can withstand a hot iron.

ENLARGING OR REDUCING DESIGNS

Enlarging or reducing your design can be easily accomplished by one of two methods.

Photocopying   The simplest technique is to take the design to your local photocopying outlet, since most modern photocopiers have an enlarging and reducing facility built in to them.

Grid   The second method uses a simple grid. Draw a grid over the original design. Then draw another grid the same size as you want the design to be, making sure that there are an equal number of squares in both the original and the second grid. Find a square on the second grid that corresponds to a square on the original and mark in all the points where the design intersects with it.

Continue in this way for all the squares and then join the marks together in the form of the original design (see Fig. 4).

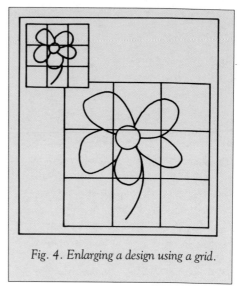

Fig. 4. Enlarging a design using a grid.

CHARTING THE DESIGN

Once you have created your design it can be useful to identify each element with the color and type of stitch you intend to use.

Using your original design on paper, assign each different stitch a number and list these at the side of the design. Then mark the design itself with the numbers.

Colors can be identified by actually coloring in the different parts of the design with the appropriate colors, or by assigning each color you intend to use with a letter and marking the design in the same way as with the numbers (see Fig. 5).

PREPARING THE THREADS

Many embroidery kits provide the threads already cut into convenient lengths. These should be placed in a thread organizer which will hold each color separate from the others

Opposite: Embroidered guest towels and washcloths.

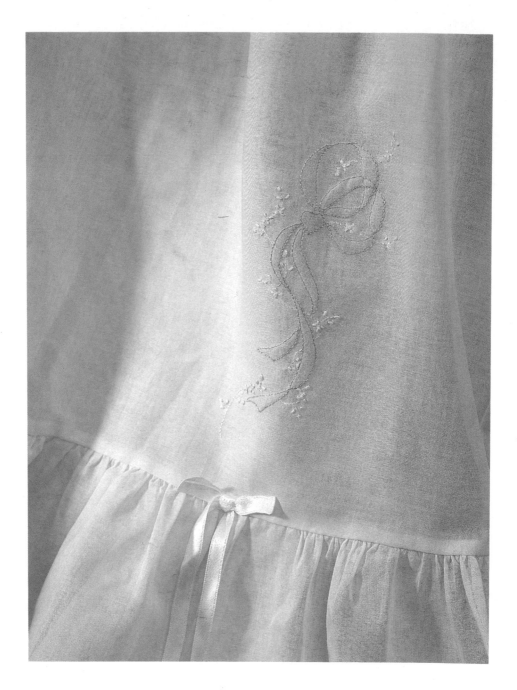

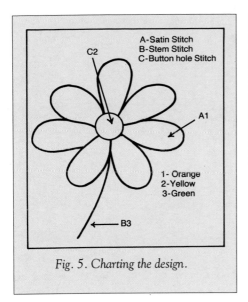

Fig. 5. *Charting the design.*

Labels in figure:
C2
A-Satin Stitch
B-Stem Stitch
C-Button hole Stitch
A1
1- Orange
2-Yellow
3-Green
B3

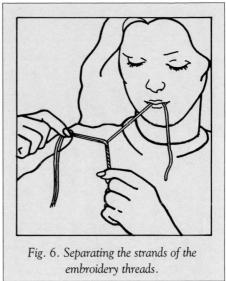

Fig. 6. *Separating the strands of the embroidery threads.*

and prevent tangling. A thread organizer is easily made from a piece of stiff cardboard or plastic into which a series of small holes have been punched along one side.

If you have purchased your thread in skeins or hanks, you will need to transfer it either to a thread organizer or bobbin. If you choose to use a thread organizer, cut the thread into lengths of no more than 15 inches. Using longer threads can mean tangles, knots and fraying (of both threads and tempers.)

If you have wound the thread onto a bobbin, you may cut the lengths as you require them. Make a note of the dye lot numbers of each skein so that you will be able to match a color if your run out.

Sometimes it will be necessary to separate the individual strands of a thread. Tease out the number of strands that you want to use from the rest of the thread at one end.

Hold one group of strands in your mouth, the other group in one hand and pull them gently apart, using your other hand to control the twisting action down the thread length. (see Fig. 6.)

Opposite: Shadework looks attractive on a fine nightgown.

TECHNIQUES OF THE CRAFT

EMBROIDERY, like all old crafts, is a very time-consuming activity and only a great deal of patience and attention to detail will result in work of high quality. If you are a beginner, do not expect to complete your work in record time, instead take extra time and care to make sure that your stitching is accurate and even, and that the tension is not too tight or too loose.

It is certainly worthwhile practicing new or particularly difficult stitches on another piece of fabric before including them in your work.

Why not consider making a sampler of different stitches? If a little thought is given to color and placement of the stitches, a sampler itself can be a very attractive piece of work and also acts as a future source of reference. Varying thread thicknesses will result in very different effects.

A stitch that looks attractive in a fine thread, for example, may lose definition when a thicker thread is used.

Before you begin to sew, think about the overall design and how each element in it relates to the others. If, for example, one part of a design appears to lie on top of another, then the lower part should be embroidered first, before the top part. This will prevent unintended glimpses of fabric between different parts of the embroidery and also adds to the realism of the design.

STARTING AND FINISHING A STITCH

The most important point to remember when starting and ending a section of stitching is *never* to use a knot to secure the thread. Knots will make the work look lumpy and will almost certainly show through if the work is mounted or framed.

To start a thread, bring the needle through the fabric from the wrong side, leaving a tail of thread about 1 inch long on the wrong side. As you embroider, make sure you work stitches over the tail thread (see Fig. 7.) If you have already begun to embroider, the new thread

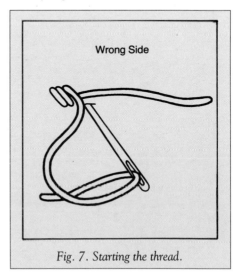

Wrong Side

Fig. 7. Starting the thread.

Opposite: Delicate embroidery is enhanced by a complementary frame.

can be tucked in behind the back of already existing stitches. To finish a thread, simply bring the needle to the back of the work and slide it behind 1 inch of completed stitches, then cut the thread (see Fig. 8). Each color should be finished off into itself, green thread behind green stitches, red thread behind red stitches and so on.

If a particular color that you are using is repeated elsewhere in the design, try and resist the temptation to carry the thread across to the new section since you run the risk of it showing through the fabric. Finish off that thread and start a new one.

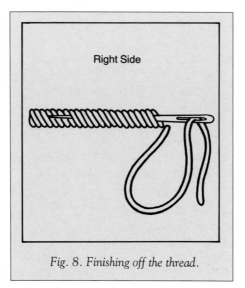

Fig. 8. Finishing off the thread.

SEWING MISTAKES

A mistake in one or two stitches can be remedied by simply unpicking those stitches.

Be careful not to pull or tug the thread; you may increase the tension on the other stitches and cause puckering.

A large area of wrong stitching is best fixed by cutting out the stitches one by one and then removing them from the wrong side of the fabric with tweezers.

Remember to secure the remaining threads.

Finely detailed feathers embroidered in gold thread.

Outline Stitches

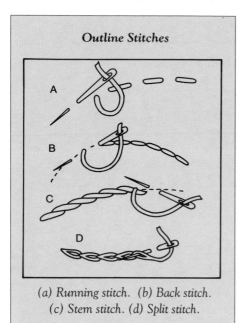

(a) Running stitch. (b) Back stitch.
(c) Stem stitch. (d) Split stitch.

Flat Stitches

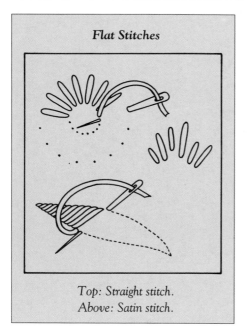

Top: Straight stitch.
Above: Satin stitch.

FREE-STYLE EMBROIDERY STITCH GUIDE

There are seven main families of stitches used in free-style embroidery: outline, flat, chain, looped, couched, knotted and filling stitches. Some of these stitches are also used in counted thread embroidery, while stitches usually seen in counted thread work can also be used for free-style embroidery, such as cross stitch. Do not be limited by the names of the stitches since one stitch can have a number of functions depending on how it is used. For example, a closely worked set of knotted stitches can function as a filling stitch, as can a series of outline stitches worked in rows.

Only a select number of stitches have been given for each stitch family and there are many other variations on these basic stitches which cannot, for reasons of space, be included in this guide. Your local library should provide you with a choice of books about embroidery which will broaden your stitch repertoire.

OUTLINE STITCHES

This group of stitches is used to outline other stitches or to define an area that is otherwise unadorned with stitching.

Running stitch

The simplest embroidery stitch, where the needle is passed over and under the fabric. Care must be taken to make each stitch the same length. Unlike most other stitches, a number of running stitches can be taken up on the needle at one time.

Back stitch

Bring the needle through onto the right side of the fabric then make a small backward stitch. Bring the needle through the fabric again, this time slightly in front of the first stitch. Take another backward stitch, inserting the needle into the point where it first came through.

Stem stitch

This stitch is worked from left to right. Take small, regular, diagonal stitches along the stitch line, making sure the thread is kept below the needle.

Split stitch

Make a small stitch over the fabric, then bring the needle back under the stitch on the wrong side of the fabric. Pierce the stitch with the needle and then make another small stitch. Continue in this manner.

FLAT STITCHES

This group of stitches is useful for filling in large areas. All stitches lie flat on the surface of the fabric.

Straight stitch

These are single stitches worked either in regular or irregular lengths. Do not make the stitches too long or loose.

Satin stitch

This stitch is simply straight stitches worked closely together. Care must be taken to insure that the stitches lie flat and that the edges of the stitches form a smooth line.

Long and short stitch

Another type of satin stitch where a long stitch is alternated with a short stitch. Use this stitch when the shape is too large to be filled with satin stitch or when a shaded effect is desired.

In the latter case, each successive row of stitches is worked in a progressively lighter (or darker) shade.

Fern stitch

Three straight stitches emerging from the same point in the fabric make up fern stitch,

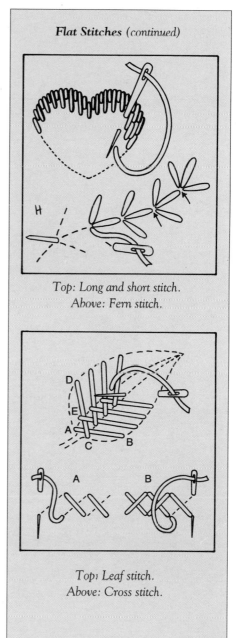

Flat Stitches (continued)

Top: *Long and short stitch.*
Above: *Fern stitch.*

Top: *Leaf stitch.*
Above: *Cross stitch.*

Above: This tablecloth
has been embroidered using mainly
satin stitch in bright colors.

Opposite: This embroidery includes
ribbons as well as thread
to create the design.

Left: An embroidered version
of Baby's Block or Tumbling Block,
a popular design with a
three-dimensional effect.

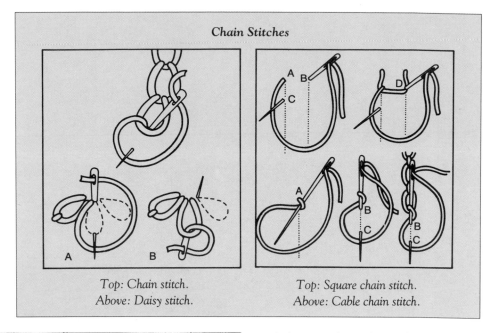

Chain Stitches

Top: *Chain stitch.*
Above: *Daisy stitch.*

Top: *Square chain stitch.*
Above: *Cable chain stitch.*

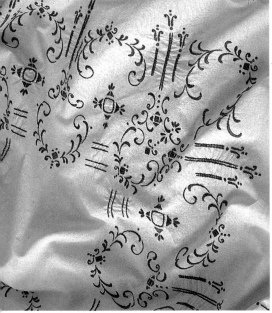

with the central straight stitch following the line of the design.

Leaf stitch

This stitch consists of overlapping, diagonal straight stitches. Follow the letter sequence to create the pattern, maintaining an even tension. An outline stitch is usually used to finish off the shape.

Cross stitch

Working from right to left, make a series of diagonal straight stitches, then reverse the direction to complete the cross. Make sure that the top half of each stitch lies in the same direction.

Left: Single color embroidery must be well designed and well executed.

CHAIN STITCHES

These stitches are used for outlining, filling and for decorative borders. As the name suggests, the stitch resembles links of a chain.

Chain stitch

To start the chain bring the thread out and hold it down with the left thumb. Re-insert the needle at the same point and make a small stitch, keeping the thread underneath the needle. Pull the thread through.

Daisy stitch

This is a single chain stitch, fastened at the base with a small stitch. Groups of this stitch can be worked in the shape of a flower.

Square chain stitch

Bring the needle out at A, insert at B directly opposite, then exit at C, keeping the thread loose and under the needle at all times. Leave enough slack so that the needle can be inserted at point D.

Cable chain stitch

Bring the needle out at A, then loop the thread over and under the needle as shown, holding the thread in place with your thumb. Insert the needle at B and bring out at C, ensuring that the thread is under the needle.

LOOPED STITCHES

Within this group, there are stitches suitable for borders, edging and filling, depending on how they are used.

Blanket stitch and buttonhole stitch

Bring the needle out at A. Insert at B and exit at C, keeping the thread under the needle. Both buttonhole and blanket stitch are worked in the same way, except that in buttonhole stitch the stitches are worked closely together to form a firm bond. Buttonhole stitch can be worked in a straight line, like blanket stitch, or in a circular fashion

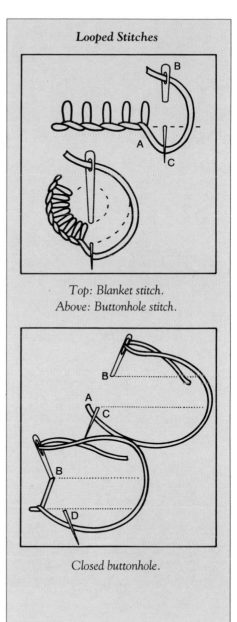

Looped Stitches

Top: *Blanket stitch.*
Above: *Buttonhole stitch.*

Closed buttonhole.

Looped Stitches (continued)

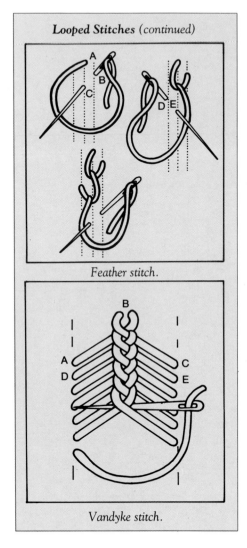

Feather stitch.

Vandyke stitch.

Right: A child's embroidered pillowcase.

Couched Stitches

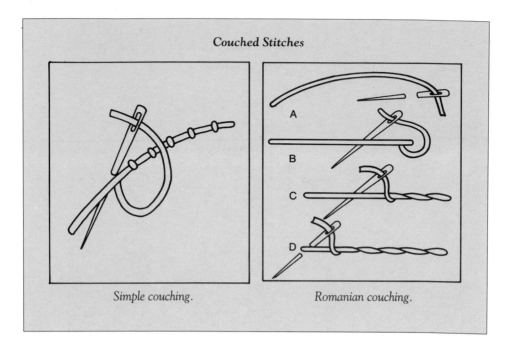

Simple couching.

Romanian couching.

as shown. Both stitches are worked from left to right.

Closed buttonhole

This is similar to buttonhole stitch except that the upright stitches are worked on the diagonal. Bring the needle out at A, insert at B and exit at C, keeping the thread under the needle. Complete the stitch by inserting at B again and exiting at D. Point D will become point A for the next stitch.

Feather stitch

In this pattern, one stitch is worked alternately on the right then the left of the center line: Bring the needle out at the center (A,) then make a stitch from B to C, keeping the thread under the needle. Repeat the same stitch, this time to the left (D to E.)

Vandyke stitch

Bring the needle through at A, make a small horizontal stitch at B then re-insert the needle at C. Bring the thread through at D then, without piercing the fabric, loop the needle under the crossed threads at B and then re-insert at E. This stitch may be used to create a leaf pattern or a braided effect, depending on the length of the side stitches.

COUCHED STITCHES

These stitches consist of two threads; the laid thread which is laid onto the fabric, and the couching thread which is used to hold the laid thread in place. Often the two threads are in contrasting colors. Couching may be used as outlining, filling or as a decorative border.

Simple couching

Lay a thread or group of threads on the fabric, following the line of your design. With needle

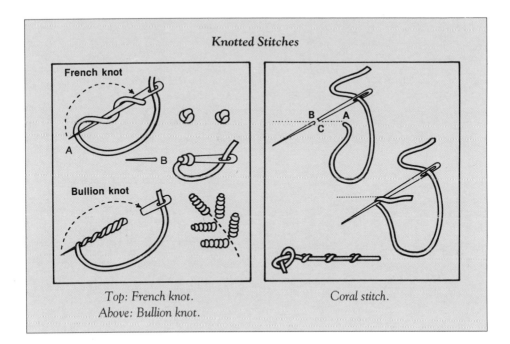

Knotted Stitches

Top: French knot.
Above: Bullion knot.

Coral stitch.

and another thread, tie down the laid thread using small stitches at regular intervals.

Romanian couching

In this type of couching, the laid and tying threads are the *same* thread. It is a useful stitch for filling large areas of fabric with a flat pattern. The laid and tied threads should be indistinguishable from each other.

KNOTTED STITCHES

These stitches have a raised appearance and are often used to create the details on flowers, the eyes of animals and so on. They are also used as filling stitches. Because they are raised, special care needs to be taken to see that they are not crushed by the embroidery hoop or squashed flat by the iron.

French knots

Bring the needle through the fabric and wrap the thread around the needle twice (see A.) Re-insert the needle at the starting point and pull through (B.) The thread should be held taut.

Bullion knots

Make a backstitch the length you want the knot to be, but do not pull the needle all the way through the fabric. Twist the thread around the needle a number of times and then pull the needle through both the fabric and the twisted thread taking care not to distort the twist. Guide the needle back to point A and re-insert.

Coral stitch

Make a small stitch, taking only a tiny, slanting stitch between B and C. Loop the thread around the needle and pull the needle through to form the knot. Continue with another stitch,

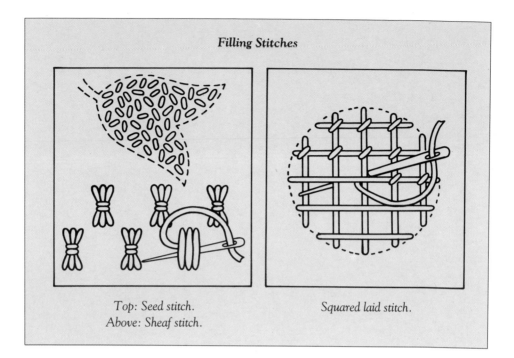

Filling Stitches

Top: *Seed stitch.*
Above: *Sheaf stitch.*

Squared laid stitch.

FILLING STITCHES

Many of the stitches already described may be used as filling stitches. Here are three more that will fill a large or small space very successfully.

Seed stitch

This stitch is simply a series of small straight stitches, worked at random over the fabric. The spacing of the stitches depends on the effect you wish to create.

Sheaf stitch

This stitch consists of three satin stitches worked from right to left, and two horizontal overcast stitches. The stitch may be worked in closely packed rows or spaced in alternate rows as shown.

Squared laid stitch

This stitch has a lattice appearance. Laid threads are placed horizontally and vertically (or diagonally) and at all points where those threads intersect, they are tied or couched, either with a small straight stitch or with a cross stitch. There are many variations of this laid filling stitch and all are very decorative.

Opposite: A modern embroidery incorporating brightly colored buttons.

FINISHING TECHNIQUES

WASHING

Unless you have been very careful to pack away your embroidery after working on it, have always had clean hands and never let anyone touch your work in progress, the finished project will probably need a wash.

If all the materials used in the embroidery are washable, use cool, soapy water and swirl the embroidery around. Avoid squeezing or wringing the fabric since this will pull the fabric and stitches out of shape.

Rinse thoroughly in a number of changes of cool water and then roll the work in a towel to absorb excess water.

If the fabric or thread is not washable it is best to send the embroidery to a reputable dry cleaners, although you should insure that the work is not pressed after cleaning as this will squash the stitches.

PRESSING

To press a piece of embroidery, the fabric should still be slightly damp. Place a folded dry towel on the ironing board and lay the embroidery face down on it.

Cover the embroidery with a pressing cloth and iron very gently, just touching the cloth. Do not exert any pressure with the iron as this may flatten the stitches.

MOUNTING

If you wish to display your embroidery on the wall, it will be necessary to mount and frame the work. The simplest method for mounting is to use a stretcher frame, like the embroidery frame discussed in the "Tools and Materials" chapter.

Four pieces of wood are mitered and glued together to form a frame and the embroidery is then stapled or nailed to it, making sure that an even tension is maintained over the entire surface. The work may then be framed.

A more sophisticated method of mounting involves placing the embroidery over a piece of board and then stretching the work by lacing it firmly at the back of the board.

If using this technique, the edges of the embroidery should be hemmed or oversewn to prevent fraying.

CARE OF EMBROIDERY

Unless you have embroidered onto a functional item such as a piece of clothing which has to be washed regularly, it is worthwhile trying to preserve the original freshness and color of your work.

Minimize exposure to direct sunlight, heat and fumes from room heaters and changes in humidity. Unless the work is behind glass, remove dust by lightly vacuuming and check for silverfish and moths.

Opposite: A Christmas placemat edged in festive gold braid.

A combination of simple embroidery stitches is used in this attractive wooden fence design.

BEGINNER'S PROJECT

THIS ATTRACTIVE WOODEN fence and flower design has been embroidered onto a piece of fabric suitable as a small tablecloth. You may think of other applications for the design, such as a table runner although, in that case, you may prefer to use the design as a border pattern rather than a central motif.

There are seven different stitches in the design which will enable you to practice and refine your embroidery techniques.

They are satin, stem, daisy, straight, back and buttonhole stitches and French knots. None of the stitches, however, are particularly difficult and all are very suitable for the embroidery beginner.

The artist has finished off the work with cotton lace as a border. Crochet, additional embroidery or a simple hem would also be suitable as finishing treatments.

MATERIALS

For a small tablecloth you will need:
- One yard of plain weave fabric, such as cotton, linen or linen-style fabric in white, cream or other neutral colors.
- Stranded cottons in the following shades, dark yellow, dusty pink, orange, burgundy red, royal blue, dark purple, medium purple, light purple, grass green, olive green, light blue, white and brown.
- You will need three skeins of brown and one skein each of the other colors.
- You will need to separate the threads into three strands for this embroidery.
- No. 7 crewel needle.
- You will also need a piece of paper and a pen for enlarging the design, tracing paper and a pencil for transferring the design and a fabric marker for marking the design onto the fabric.

METHOD
Step One
- Wash and press the fabric and hem the edges to prevent any fraying.
- Finger-press the center folds into the fabric.
- Sort the threads into the thread organizer.

Step Two
- The design is repeated four times to create a square with cut corners.
- Corner motif uses the snapdragon element of the full design.
- The design will need to be enlarged from the size it appears in this book.
- Using the design (see Fig. 9) and technique given in the "Starting Work" chapter, enlarge so that each square side measures: 11 inches in length by 2 1/2 inches at its highest point, with the corner motifs measuring; 3 inches x 2 inches.

Placement of the design is shown in Fig. 10.

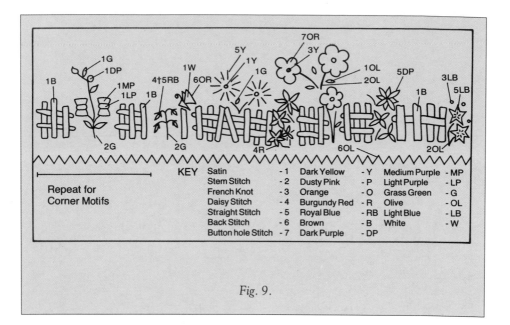

KEY

Stitch		Color			
Satin	- 1	Dark Yellow	- Y	Medium Purple	- MP
Stem Stitch	- 2	Dusty Pink	- P	Light Purple	- LP
French Knot	- 3	Orange	- O	Grass Green	- G
Daisy Stitch	- 4	Burgundy Red	- R	Olive	- OL
Straight Stitch	- 5	Royal Blue	- RB	Light Blue	- LB
Back Stitch	- 6	Brown	- B	White	- W
Button hole Stitch	- 7	Dark Purple	- DP		

Repeat for
Corner Motifs

Fig. 9.

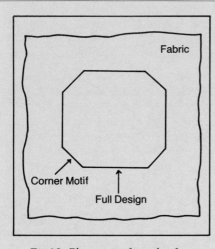

*Fig 10. Placement of wooden fence
and flower design.*

Step Three

- Making sure it is centered, trace the design onto the fabric and then, using the color and stitch key in Fig. 9, you may begin to embroider.
- Apart from the back palings of the fence, which should be embroidered first since they are the lowest part of the design, there is no particular embroidery sequence to follow.
- Finish off the edges in one of the treatments suggested, wash and press carefully, and your embroidered tablecloth is complete.

INDEX

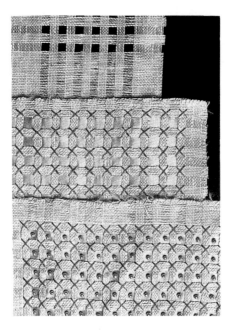

Two steps of embroidery technique
showing the completed piece with beads.